'Paperchains is a wo
have been thrilled th

Creativity lies at the very heart of our industry and, in
what has been an unprecedented time for so many
people, families and organisations both here in the
UK and around the world, it is great to have been
involved in an initiative that shines the light on voices
that are often less heard, capturing the spirit of lockdown in an uplifting way.'

David Austin, Chief Executive, BBFC

'Paperchains is unfettered alchemy in dire times. It has
ignited positivity in those it has touched. It is a
domino effect of artistic perfection, provoked by
oblivion in the benevolent spirit of Brooke, Sassoon,
and Owen.'

Ian Thornton, Novelist and Producer

'The greatest human connectors are words—but sometimes getting your words heard is almost impossible. Paperchains is a brilliant conduit for the words of those who rarely get heard.'

Erwin James, Inside Time and The Guardian

'It's clear many people's voices are marginalised in the UK. Paperchains is one way to help create a polyphony we can be proud of.'

Tom Palmer, writer

Paperchains

Our Stories from Lockdown

Edited by Sam Ruddock
Foreword by Stephen Kelman
Introduction by David Kendall and A.G. Smith
Afterword by Nell Leyshon

**Story
Machine**

Paperchains, Copyright Story Machine , 2021

Print ISBN: 9781912665129
Ebook ISBN: 9781912665136
Published by Story Machine,
130 Silver Road, Norwich, NR3 4TG
storymachines.co.uk

Set in Garamond; used under licence.

Printed and bound in the UK by Seacourt Ltd

Story Machine is committed to the environment.
This book is printed using processes that are:

100% carbon positive **100%** EMAS **100%** renewable energy **100%** ISO14001 **100%** eco-friendly simitri® toner **100%** recycled FSC® stock

Zer0 % waste to landfill

Printed by **seacourt** – proud to be counted amongst the top environmental printers in the world

Paperchains

Our Stories from Lockdown

Contents

Foreword

When my friend Alan texted me in April 2020 to say that he was working on a project in response to the COVID-19 pandemic, and the national lockdown that had begun the previous month, none of us had any idea that, over a year later, life would still be so restricted and uncertain. But Alan, and David Kendall, co-founders of Paperchains, know all about restriction and uncertainty, having spent their professional lives in prisons and Young Offenders Institutions, and working with homeless people, and young people in care. Paperchains was created to ensure that those people's voices – people who would end up suffering most acutely from the isolation that lockdown imposed – were heard. A means of sharing their experiences, and contributing as equals to the record of a national event that has affected us all.

When we come to look back on the Coronavirus years, it is important that nobody's perspective is excluded. Since April 2020, Paperchains has been collecting submissions from up and down the country. From the heartrending to the hilarious, the satirical to the sublime, and every point between, the stories, poems, essays and artworks that flooded in from prisoners and other marginalised groups provided an invaluable insight into how things were for them during this unprecedented time. That insight will go a long way towards bridging the considerable gap between society's perception of its forgotten citizens and their reality. It is a reality I have been invited into as part of my own work alongside Alan, visiting prisons and Young Offenders Institutions under the auspices of Books Unlocked, a programme run by the National Literacy Trust and the Booker Prize Foundation designed to bring literature to places where its capacity to enlighten and transform can be most powerfully felt.

There is nothing more damaging than a voice silenced, and nothing more wonderfully productive than a voice unlocked; this anthology is a testament to the belief that by telling our stories we learn not only to understand ourselves but to understand each other. A story is a vehicle for empathy, a delivery system for love, and we will need these things more than ever in the post-COVID world, where the inequalities that have defined our society for so long will be exposed as never before. What kind of world we get to live in will be determined largely by our willingness to reject easy prejudices about our fellow citizens and instead to assume the best of them. Only by working together will we survive and flourish.

The contents of this anthology can be read as individual reports from the frontline of the first national lockdown: personal accounts of fear and hope, despair and determination, worry and wonder. They made me laugh and cry and re-evaluate what I think and believe. Together, these accounts form an alternative collective memory as real and beautiful as any from the so-called mainstream. A memory of a time none of us wish to relive, yet a time we can all take lessons from, if we choose to. So read, and enjoy, and ponder, and then ask yourself: what did I learn when the world got sick, and what can I do to make it better?

Stephen

Introduction

HMP&YOI Brinsford Library. Monday 23rd March, 2020

'Can you catch it from books boss?'

In thirteen years working in prison libraries I've heard many questions. But this is a first. On a different day I might have answered with a joke; but today isn't a different day.

I am aware of the underlying tension in the room and it's reflected in the face of the man in front of me.

'I don't think so.' I answer truthfully, but before I hand him the book I clean the cover with an anti-bacterial wipe.

Over the radio we hear a request for officer assistance in another area of the prison. Then a second burst of static followed by an announcement of a standing roll check. Prison life carrying on as usual and I'm reminded of a passage in H.G. Well's The War of the Worlds

'It seems to me now almost incredibly wonderful that, with that swift fate hanging over us, men could go about their petty concerns as they did.'

The day carries on like any other Monday, except that by eight o'clock that evening we are all sitting down to watch the Prime Minister's announcement. In one life-changing moment all the invisible strings that have held us up are cut away. We're left floundering.

The next day I learn I'm amongst the fortunate ones. I can work from home. See out the pandemic from a safe place. Going on with my life whilst others, quite literally, are now stepping in to frontline hell. The only emotion I feel at this point is guilt. There has been no time to prepare. No time to put anything in place to help my prison community. I wondered whether, if human contact had suddenly become a threat, how we could safely reach out to help those who needed it the most? After all, when there is physical separation we can still be linked through creativity.

Several years ago I faced a serious illness and during that period I felt separated from those around me. On one hand life had continued as normal, but I no longer felt part of the world – almost as though I were looking at it through a hazy mirror. My creative voice hadn't been lost, but I felt as though no one was listening anymore. I told myself, why would someone want to ruin their day hearing my story?

The physical scars of that time may have faded now but the mental ones will always remain. I'm glad, because they are the reason I couldn't bury that feeling of guilt at now being safe and do nothing. From that feeling, the idea of Paperchains was born.

David and I discussed Paperchains within days of the first announcement of the UK Lockdown. In essence the idea was a simple one. We form a chain of words, poetry and art that binds us all together. A chain that will survive beyond this turbulent time and stand as a testament of who we were during it. What we were thinking, feeling, striving and surviving for. Something that future generations will study as they try to understand what this time must have been like for those who lived through it.

We needed to hear the voices being stifled by the pandemic. Those people who have always had a voice but were now struggling to find an audience for it. Those of us who are dealing with addiction, prison or life on the streets. Armed Forces personnel deployed away from family, and the young people within all these extraordinary communities.

The anthology you are reading is testament to all the people who have worked to make Paperchains happen. Thanks to visionaries like Sam Ruddock of Story Machine and a vanguard of supporters who immediately recognised the worth of the project, Paperchains has become an acclaimed success.

A quarter of the prisons across the UK took part alongside our Homeless and Armed Forces families. Every single entrant received a personal letter of thanks and a Paperchains wristband.

Paperchains has now become a part of history. It exists as an incredible showcase of talent both as a book and as a theatrical production that retells the story of these exceptional people and ensures that we will all keep listening.

We are also delighted that the Mass Observation Archive will become the home of all the Paperchains submissions, were they can be stored and studied for generations to come.

All of you who joined Paperchains should be proud. Its success is of your making.

Keep safe and keep creating because tomorrow doesn't have to be yesterday.

Alan and David

Breath

Difficulty breathing?
Not from Coronavirus
But lack of fresh air

Locked in a cell
24/7
The pair of us
It's the size of your bathroom
One on the other
On top of each other

It's the stench
The sweaty smell of
Our unwashed bodies
Seven days running

Locked up
In the matchbox room
In and Out
We breathe
We inhale and exhale
Over and over again
The same recycled air
The stench of our unwashed bodies
Almost suffocating
And yet not

Simon

Locked Up in Lockdown

I have been in Hydebankwood Secure College for almost four years now. At the beginning of my time here in 2017 I was a drug addict, unsettled, angry and still trying to come to terms with the very serious crime I committed.

During my first two years here I broke the rules, participated in drug use, got into fights and had an extremely negative opinion of prison staff (screws). As a result, that time in here felt like a lifetime. I spent the majority of my days locked up, angry, and blaming everyone else but myself. In October of 2018 I decided to participate in The Headway Landing. This Landing was voluntary and the aim of this project was to break down barriers between staff and prisoner, and to challenge negative behaviour.

After only a week I asked to move back to a normal landing again. I was struggling with being challenged and I didn't want to engage positively with staff. However, the regular staff there talked me out of it and encouraged me to try and engage positively. It was at this stage in my life that it dawned on me: staff are just like the rest of us and maybe it was worthwhile trying to make the most of it. Finally, the penny had dropped.

It was only in February 2020 that I made it to the ultimate enhanced landing (C5) which is where people who are working hard, keeping their head down, and are drug-free can reside. It is a hard earned privilege to make it to this level of trust and enhancement. The landing has a number of perks including a late lock up of 11pm, an outside food shop, a fully furnished kitchen with oven and hob where you can make your own food. It also has an upgraded bedroom and living area, and you are given more trust and freedom than any other students within the centre.

After only five weeks of enjoying the 'luxury' of this enhancement Covid-19 struck. I was moved off and told I had to reside on a shielded landing due to asthma making me high risk of Covid-19.

This shielded landing is just like being back at square one for me. It is the same landing I resided on as a new committal on arrival at Hydebank. It almost seems like a punishment to be asthmatic at this time. All my hard work and determination now feels wasted. I am now stuck on the landing at all times, back to 7pm lock up, basic facilities, no gym and limited time outside. To be put back to these basics from the late lock-up, a job morning and afternoon, and more freedom, feels like a kick in the teeth.

On arrival to the shielded landing I entered my new cell which was very unclean. The walls were covered in toothpaste where the last person had stuck photos up, the floor was badly marked and the counters dirty with cigarette ash. It all felt overwhelming. I didn't know where to begin, or who to turn to. I sat on the bed with my head in my hands.

The only other person on this landing at the time was deaf and I began to feel guilty for feeling lonely. The visits in the centre had been stopped to try and prevent the coronavirus spreading and this was a very big challenge for me as I was used to seeing my family every week. I noticed then that my mental health was declining and I was worried I would spiral out of control, back to the old me. I spoke with mental health and kept myself busy in an attempt to distract me from overthinking.

Soon enough virtual visits were set up online meaning I could see all my family. This was a really enjoyable experience for me getting to see our family home, dog, and other family members who rarely get to come and visit. The shielded landing now has a job in horticulture and I enjoy getting out every day to water the plants, do some weeding and general maintenance. When the sun is out, we also get some time to breathe in the fresh air, feel the heat on our skin, relax and clear the head. As much as I would love to be back on C5 I have now accepted that this is the safest place for me at this time. I have settled with the company of the other students who are now residing on the landing and am presently being taught sign language so that I may communicate better with my new friend.

I know that when times are safer, I will return to the landing and the privileges I have earned.

Michael

Arrival

Along came Coronavirus
And folks started to take heed
Running out to get what essentials
They were all going to need

Head Office sent out the pastor
To forgive us all of our sin
But sadly this was a journey in vain
'Cos the poor bloke couldn't get in.

Shirley

Lockdown: 30 Years On

Lockdown: NOUN
- a state of isolation or restricted access instituted as a security measure.
- the confining of prisoners to their cells, typically in order to regain control during a riot.

Lockdown 2020: Day 50
Lunchtime.

It's such a lovely day today I think I'll have lunch in the garden. I'm so lucky to have the garden; having to shield due to my underlying health issues can be really tiresome at times but when I think of those living in tower blocks, with no garden, no balcony even; irritable, bored kids to deal with and no-where to go, I feel very thankful for what I do have. And I think of those on their own, reliant on family and friends if they have them. It's tough times for a lot of people at the moment in so many ways, socially, emotionally, psychologically.

It is a bit different since the last time I was on lockdown, 30 years ago. That was when Strangeways kicked off and loads of UK nicks went up in sympathy with the lads there. I was in a maximum security prison near York at the time. What a nightmare that was. I wonder if lockdown in the nick is the same today? I'd have thought if anything it would be even worse…staffing and funding has gone through the floor over the past 30 years while prisoner numbers have gone up along with the violence and self-harm. I can't help but feel for them, all those men, women and children under lockdown in our prisons at this moment, as I write.

Lockdown 1990: Day 5

Lunchtime.

Well, it should be but goodness knows when I'll get it. 150 lads on this wing and controlled unlock on lockdown means only 2 unlocked at a time to get their food. Takes bloody forever. I only got my breakfast 90 minutes ago, 2 hours later than usual…a stone cold half a grilled tomato and a slice of cardboard toast that must have seen the grill 4 hours previously. I was tempted to have the slice of bread I'd kept from tea yesterday but I'll be far hungrier by the end of the day so I'll save it till then; I've still got the blob of marge from breakfast to have it with.

23 hour bang up in a 7 foot by 8 foot stone box with a thick steel door with no handle on the inside; bloody hell, it could drive you

*mad. Adam across the landing is kicking
seven bells out of his door again…BANG,
BANG, BANG constant; he can hardly
keep it together at the best of times but this
bang up is really doing his head in. Thing is,
you've got no idea when it's your turn to be
unlocked. You get a clue when you hear the
screws start on your landing, but I can't hear
them yet. Could be 2 minutes, could be 2
hours. Drives you mad…and I'm hungry;
everyone's always hungry in this nick. You
don't expect 5 Star Cordon Bleu but the
food's shite here.*

I'll make myself a tuna sandwich today. Lockdown's
given me the chance to get into my breadmaking, getting
creative with different flours and ingredients. I'm really
pleased with my latest one: 25% rye flour, 25% whole-
meal and 50% white. I've also added some sunflower
seeds, linseeds, a good sprinkle of dried mixed herbs and
some finely milled almonds. This has created a dense,
heavy bread with a natural smell and close texture.

I'll cut a generously thick slice and carefully coat it in
olive oil and buttermilk spread; then make a bed of baby
spinach leaves as a base upon which I'll sprinkle some
salt and cracked black pepper.

I prefer tuna in sunflower oil…it lends a rich

moistness to the fish that I like. I'll drain most, but not all, of the oil off and keep it to drizzle over Harvey the dog's food later on – he loves that. The great thing about the bed of spinach on the bread is that I can keep the tuna quite moist with the oil but it won't make the bread go soggy. I'll put the tuna in a bowl and then finely chop one of those lovely large, firm vine ripened tomatoes; by chopping it so finely then the juice of the tomato will be much more easily absorbed by the tuna when I mix them together.

Again, give it a good twist of black pepper to lend it some bite along with some chopped thyme, mint and basil from our herb garden then mix it all together before carefully spooning it over the bread and spinach leaves to create a wholesome and filling open sandwich to enjoy, washed down with a long cold drink, sat in the garden, on this lovely sunny day.

I'm so aware I would not now appreciate the liberty I currently have to enjoy such a delicious, simple pleasure had I not gone through lockdown 30 years ago.

An hour later and still no lunch, no sound of the screws out there. I think they might be on the landing below. If they are then my best guess is it's going to be at least another half an hour.

But that landing down there, where the screws

are at the moment, that's one of the no go areas in this place…it's dangerous to go down there if you've no business to be there because it's been colonised by the Essex gangsters, the professional villains and even the screws know you don't mess with them. They'll be unlocked for their lunch, 2 at a time, and they'll take their time, just to make a point that this unlock only goes off smoothly with the consent of the cons. So they'll take their time, they'll refill their water jugs from the recess, they'll say I'll just pass this paper to me mate, Boss, and slide it under their door, and they'll have a natter for as long as they feel they can get away with it and sod everyone else waiting for their lunch. Actually, it's probably going to be another hour till I get something.

And despite myself, I can sense I'm getting really wound up now but that's pointless. Start kicking off and you'll just get told to keep it down or else…and they may even just decide to leave you till last anyway just for the laff , just to wind you up more, and they'll be ready and waiting to jump on you if you kick off when they do finally open the door. It's all part of

the game in here… They've been serving now
for a couple of hours; the hotplate that keeps
the food warm is on a timer to save money…I
hope the food stays hot enough to eat once I get
it.

Our garden's very natural, not one of those finely mani-
cured and ordered creations; lots of shrubs, grasses, the
herb garden and this small patch of lawn, sat here in the
sun, eating my tuna sandwich, Harvey begging for a bite
and blackbirds, magpies, sparrows and jays singing their
songs.

In such peace, it's very difficult sometimes to grasp
the grave seriousness of this pandemic, the toll it's taking;
people dying before their time, families grieving, such
loss. The economic cost – the loss of jobs, those on
furlough, confronted for the first time with the vagaries
of a benefits system that grinds soooo slowly. And in the
meantime, the mortgage or the rent is being missed, the
struggle even for the food on the table when times were
hard enough anyway before all this. The strain on rela-
tionships, the shouting at the kids, the fighting with your
partner, the loss of regular routine causing a deep and
dangerous insecurity in the minds and hearts of house-
holds and communities across the globe, not just round
here.

It's good that the mental health cost of these things
on folk is recognised by the authorities, that there are to

be accessed if necessary the helplines and websites; there's family, friends, Zoom, Skype for those with all or some of those supports; many ways to try to ease the pressure we feel at times, the burden, the worry, the anxiety, the sheer not knowing what the future will bring. And this, on top of the worry about health and when, if, things will ever go back to how they were...

Adam's still kicking the life out of his door across the landing and some of the lads are getting really hacked off now, shouting abuse at the screws, kicking the door, playing music full blast to drown out the anger in their head....bloody bedlam you can't hear yourself think and it grates on your nerves and on and on and on and on...; I'm pacing up and down my cell here...still no sign of lunch, 90 minutes late, I'm bloody hungry and I bet the food's going to be bloody cold by the time I get it.

How the hell's teeth are you supposed to keep it together, stuck in this stone box of a cell, 23 hour bang up, constant vague sense of hunger and no-one gives a monkeys...just suck it up because if you don't and you kick off, you'll just be dragged off to the punishment block and left to stew in your own misery and nursing a couple of bruises for good measure just to remind you who's boss.

I'm 7 years into my life sentence, God knows how many to go. I know why I'm here, I know what I did but this ain't right. This ain't humane. And where's my ##### LUNCH? I'M HUNGRY!'

I'll take Harvey out for his lunchtime walk now, which can also be my permitted once a day walk. It's fantastic that we back onto a sports field here and a short walk away is the country park reclaimed from the old coal mine complex that closed in the late 1990's. Surrounded by fresh air, the glories of nature, that sense of freedom and open space…

It's such a blessing, this being able to get out. There's so many who can't at the moment, so many who must feel everything falling apart and the trauma for many people is and will be immeasurable. Thankfully, there's talk now of lockdown easing, a phased opening up of things again, giving us at least a glimmer of hope that things won't always be like this.

But things will never be the way they were again it seems to me. Even when lockdown eases, the challenges that people will face, the trials our communities will face in the nation as a whole will be enormous. There's a Perfect Storm brewing it seems…environmental catastrophe, deepening social fragmentation, looming economic hardship, ongoing political discord; and the virus hasn't gone away and there's no vaccine yet, and all that even before Brexit really kicks in at year's end.

Are these the last days in lockdown? No wonder the UK's mental health is deteriorating, that ordinary decent folk are beginning to glimpse just how ephemeral are what we once imagined as our certainties. Thank God we at least have our liberty; to see and enjoy the colours of nature, the touch of the breeze, the voice of our family, the support of our friends, the simple joy of a tuna sandwich, how you like it, when you want it. Surely it is these simple yet precious gifts that will keep us sane in the days ahead. God help us, Friend of all we weak and helpless creatures.

And especially those in prison. God help them, Friend of all Your weak and helpless creatures; I hope and pray it's better for them today than it was in my day.

Oh for crying out loud, now it's raining!
Exercise will be cancelled and we won't even
get the hour out of our cell today; 24 hours
bang up…I'm cracking up here, how long
are we supposed to live like this, how on
earth do they think we can keep it together?
At last, the screws are on our landing and I
think I'll be next for lunch, over two hours
after it's supposed to come and please God

don't let them unlock Adam with me, I can't take his anger on board I've got enough problems keeping myself together.

The hotplate at the servery is cold as I brush past it; I just hope there's still enough heat left in the food to make it edible. I look at my tray as I take it back to my cell. Some sort of stew, grey with all the flour used to thicken it up; the mash with the black lumps from the frostbitten potatoes the prison gets because they can't be put into supermarkets; the cabbage stewed to an off-white mush.

I get back to my cell and the screw slams the door behind me. It's cold. The food is cold. It's stone cold. IT'S ##### COLD!! ; in my hunger, my despair, my anger, I watch it slide down my cell wall into which I've just hurled it and so I too descend further, one day deeper into my deteriorating mental health, feeling like a ticking time bomb.

And this is only Day 5. God, please help us, Friend of we weak and the helpless creatures.

WHERE IS PRISONS EXIT STRATEGY?

Keeping prisoners locked up 23 hours a day for months on end is turning prisons into 'ticking time bombs', Labour's Shadow Justice Secretary David Lammy warns. The lockdown in jails to curb coronavirus could damage residents' mental health and lead to tensions, conflict, and unrest.

Inside Time: 31st May 2020

Jed

Emptiness

While others use days of quarantine constructively, I use my working from home time to research the grunge bands of Seattle from the late 80's. Three days into this new obsession I begin to feel a new hole, an ache on the inside. The whirl of guitars, that sound, that drone, the noise that only a heroin addict can hear.

My eyes grow heavy with memory. My mouth opens bending at the sides and my head tilts back softly as I listen. There is no wave beneath me holding my body from falling into a waiting early grave. The guitars don't sound like the music wants it to. The fluffy tar clouds in heaven don't call to cushion me. I am falling and there is nothing to soften the blow.

But I am sober and I can't hear the sound. The world has its brakes on and my days are like my days of old. I have no responsibilities and no reason to get up. Oblivion costs ten pound and lives on the empty streets of Boscombe Crescent.

I dream of Lexington with poets past, Seattle with dead grunge gods, Texas with the ghosts of outlaw folk musicians. I am no longer excited by being free and detoxified. I take sleeping tablets but the music doesn't sound the same.

Quarantine holds no weight, I have been preparing for this for years and hell has always been more appealing to me.

People often ask me what heroin feels like. That is the whole point; it feels like nothing.

Shelley

The New Normal

Listen!
It's birdsong
Not cars or planes
Just nature.
Everything's changed

Now we are all prisoners
Our cells are our homes
Your homes become cells
Maybe now you understand

Social distance is hard to maintain
On the exercise yard
that precious hour to get daily fresh air

Another new death toll on the TV
Announced by a politician.

Is this the new normal?
The world at a standstill,
trapped by this virus

Anonymous

Headlines

Coronavirus
Infects civilisations
And their news channels

Xavier

LOCKDOWN: A STRUCTURAL CHANGE

Following the Prime Minister's instructions to Stay At Home, HMP Blackstock is left to fend for itself. Staff are refusing to work and in order to keep their community safe from Covid-19, the residents at Blackstock have elected three residential leaders.

HMP Blackstock has been transformed into a place of intense productivity, moral judgements are ever-present, and a new way of life enhances current regulations.

Meanwhile, in parliament, the Justice Secretary is held accountable. The thought of military intervention is being toyed with by the Prime Minister. Will anarchy ensue, or will trusting the convicts triumph? Sit back and enjoy the twists and turns of the Criminal Justice System.

CHARACTERS

PRIME MINISTER (PM). The man in charge of the country is a white, middle-aged, middle-class gentleman with a strong dislike of marginalised communities He understands the importance of demonising the lower classes and has a particular anger towards those who contravene the legislation set by him and his comrades. Although he is set in his ways, he is susceptible to change.

JUSTICE SECRETARY. The Prime Minister's under-study is an inexperienced 28-year-old black male who is sympathetic towards those he represents. Wanting change, but not quite influential enough, the Blackstone issue is welcomed by the Justice Secretary. His devil's advocate approach with the Prime Minister is a deliberate ploy to influence change. Could the Secretary's cunningness change the way in which justice is achieved?

PRISON SPOKESPERSON (Spokesperson) . The man tasked with running the prison is a 32-year-old white working-class male with a military background. He is a charismatic leader and the length of time he has spent behind bars has given him an in-depth understanding of what works for those in prison. All decisions made are done with a moral judgement, no decision is taken lightly, and a utilitarianism approach often prevails.

JOURNALIST JOHN (JJ). JJ is a clumsy journalist, his unorthodox style leaves many professionals avoiding his questions. He appears to be ill-prepared while he is on air. His quickness however, allows him to put three square meals on his children's plates. John has been married for 14 years, and his early marriage (18) allowed his wife to control affairs at home, while he is the bread-winner.

SCENE 1
HMP Blackstock, Exterior, present day

ALERT! News has surfaced that staff at HMP Blackstock are refusing to go to work for fear of catching Covid19 which has left the prison being run by the residents. Journalists are following the story!

JOURNALIST JOHN Give me the nod when we are on air.
And action

Good morning ladies and gentlemen, we have an extraordinary story unfolding in front of our very eyes. You join us outside HMP Blackstock, where we believe that three inmates have taken on the task of running the prison. The stay-at-home message did not apply to prison staff, but those who actually run this place are taking no risks. It's truly extraordinary. I've been Journalist John and we'll keep you updated on this revelation.

SCENE 2
No.10 Downing Street interior, present day

PRIME MINISTER   What on earth are you doing to rid this problem at Blackstock? This is damaging our ability to run the country, we are losing confidence and god knows what's going on inside that petulant prison. Have you contacted the Military?

JUSTICE SEC   Sir, I'm not sure sending in the army will bring back public confidence. We cannot simply use troops to regain our prison, we will look like aggressors invading an innocent bunch of shoplifters.

PRIME MINISTER   Innocent! Those toerags are not innocent. Remember who the enemy was before Covid. If it isn't Covid destroying our economy, it's those reprobates sponging off the state and over-using legal aid fees. We need this sorted and we need it sorted now.

JUSTICE SEC   Calm down Prime Minister, calm down. I have already put an ad on social media for new staff. Before

we know it, we will recruit hun-
dreds of school leavers to run the
prison. We've done this before.

PRIME MINISTER   Yes, but let's face it we have never
had an invisible killer ripping
through our streets. This is bonk-
ers. I am trying to run the country
and restore faith in the British
people, and all I'm hearing is the
fear that Blackstock will soon be
empty and our streets will have
more problems. Oh you've got to
be kidding!

SCENE 3
No.10 Downing Street interior, present day

*The Prison Spokesperson addresses the nation from HMP Black-
stock through a virtual hearing, the Prime Minister and Justice
Secretary watch.*

SPOKESPERSON   We are experiencing turbulent
times, our world is under threat.
We are, however, acutely aware
that many of you will be anxious
with the changes occurring in

HMP Blackstock. We would like to address the nation and inform them of some fundamental changes that are planned under this new management.

We hope that our transparency will ease public anxiety and help us to build a trustworthy relationship with our community.

PRIME MINISTER   What on earth is happening? Get this cretin off the air. If we haven't lost the public's confidence already, we have now! We are risking everything here, it has taken us years to feed the public the image that prisoners are scum and feeble-minded, this press conference goes totally against that

SPOKESPERSON   Our first and critical announcement is that the gates at HMP Blackstock will remain closed until Covid-19 is no longer in circulation, protecting our residents' health is vital but allowing them to continue with their rehabilitation is paramount to a successful reintegration. With their rehabilitation in mind, as of today, all residents who engage in purposeful activity will receive a national minimum wage. Slavery is abolished from this day onwards.

PRIME MINISTER   I beg your pardon, I hope they don't think they'll be using the taxpayer's money to fund this, we already have 80% of the population being pampered on the furlough scheme, never mind funding these animals.

SPOKESPERSON   This announcement will no doubt come as a shock to many law-abiding citizens whom are struggling, but we can assure you that it is a sacrifice worth taking. Increased productivity will improve skills and experience, which in turn will reduce re-offending. You my friends will not have to worry about the residents returning to your communities. We hope that this conference has been useful for those with doubts on how Blackstock is being run. We have good intentions and will endeavour to reform our characters I must however, finish on a word of caution.

It has been noticed that a resident under our care has flouted the rules and escaped from Blackstock. He is heading for the County Durham area and he also has ties to the Barnard Castle area. Do not approach this individual, we will keep your informed.

SCENE 4
HMP Blackstock exterior, present day

JJ

As you can see I am standing outside HMP Blackstock. If the story unfolding in front of us wasn't crazy enough, we are going to see more inmates released today I wonder which lucky devil is next. Wait, the gates are opening. Would you just look at that! Excuse me sir, excuse me. Can we have a quick word with you before you go and loot the streets? Argh, I'm

sorry that was the wrong reel,
what's happening here?

EX-PRISONER   Well, the managers have decided
to take the term Preparation for
Release by its literal meaning, as
you can see I have a car on its
way out.

JJ   A car?

EX-PRISONER   Yes, I've been assembling this
from scratch in the motor me-
chanics workshop. We repair
cars, get them road safe and we
keep them for release.

JJ   Now that's a bit of kit. We've
also been hearing that you lot in
there are getting the national
minimum wage, go on then
show us the dosh.

EX-PRISONER   I've managed to save five grand,
this will go on a deposit for a
flat. Right I'm going to shoot on
now, I have a Mrs to return to.

JJ   One last question, who can we
expect out next?

EX-PRISONER

My guess is that all those detained unlawfully on the indeterminate public protection sentences are those on Joint Enterprise laws. The injustices are being dealt with first.

JJ

There you have it, you heard it here first, the calm before the storm. We're not moving an inch, surely we are due a riot. I've been Journalist John, live at HMP Blackstock.

SCENE 5
No.10 Downing Street interior, present day

The Prime Minister readies himself for another briefing coming out of Blackstock.

PRIME MINISTER

What disaster story are we going to hear now? Either Covid's riddled the prison, or they have killed one another, whatever the outcome I am still in favour of military intervention.

SPOKESPERSON

Good afternoon ladies and

gentlemen and welcome to HMP Blackstock's daily briefing. Before we address the changes we have made here, we would like to update you on the worrying story we left you with yesterday. As we highlighted one of the residents sadly took off from Blackstock, but we are glad to announce that this individual has been located and returned to Blackstock. Following his 14 days isolation period, this individual will address his community. As a result of his 200-mile trip we have investigated this potential breach. We believe that this individual was acting reasonably and responsibly and that all residents would act in a similar fashion if the opportunity arose. A man has needs and we believe that his basic instinct allowed him to act rationally. However, it has come to light that this individual enjoyed a second trip and this will not be tolerated.

PRIME MINISTER   As repugnant as this story is, I am interested to find out the punishment. If that was one of mine I would… Well in fairness this is not about me, let's move on.

SPOKESPERSON I would like to finish by sharing a change in the regime here at Blackstock. We are delighted to announce the transformation of a residential unit into a university campus. The physical environment is under reconstruction, non-Wi-Fi laptops are being installed and shared accommodation is on its way. Prison, by its very nature holds residents with a wealth of talent and knowledge, and we intend to take full advantage of this Residents will learn academic subjects from their peers, they will be encouraged to cook for one another and have weekly assignments set. That concludes today's briefing

SCENE 6
No.10 Downing Street interior, the future

Three months in, a vaccine is now available, the Prime Minister addresses the country with the good news then debates what he is going to do about Blackstock.

PRIME MINISTER   Today is a special day, the time has come where we can celebrate, we have a vaccine! I would like to thank my ministers for leading this campaign against such a dangerous enemy. I would like to extend my thanks to the scientific advisors for their guidance. But more importantly, I would like to thank you, the British people for showing such resolve during difficult and uncertain times. This has been a national effort and together we have prevented millions more fatalities. You should truly remain proud of yourselves and when the next generation looks back in history, they will truly view their loved ones as heroes Yes, I said it, heroes! Thank you.

The Prime Minister turns away from the camera to his colleagues

PRIME MINISTER   Right, let's now address the elephant in the office, what on

	earth are we going to do about Blackstock?

JUSTICE SEC   It s worth noting Prime Minister that those who have been re-leased from Blackstock, well not one of them have returned to prison, not one of them have reoffended, and they seem to be doing just fine.

PRIME MINISTER   The authorities have been watching them closely, they must have done something. A burgla-ry of a theft, what about their rent, are they up to date?

JUSTICE SEC   You would think so wouldn't you? These lot are not only staying out but they're on the ladder now, and they've got well paid jobs. The rumour is we might be sharing our House with one of these ex-lags sooner than we think. John Pike, ex-Blackstock lag, is running for Blackpool North and the polls suggest he is favourite.

PRIME MINISTER   And there's no backlash?

JUSTICE SEC   It's quite the opposite Prime
                Minister The journalists have
                been distracted with Covid so
                without their demonisation of
                criminals, public opinion has
                changed. And, with the saga in
                Blackstock, people are proving
                quite forgiving towards those
                with convictions

PRIME MINISTER I knew times were changing, but
                I never thought I'd witness a
                love-a-con era. I have heard
                enough Martin, pass me the
                phone

The Prime Minister makes a phone call to the Director of Prisons in the South.

PRIME MINISTER John, I need a favour, locate me
                the last 12 offenders released
                from Blackstock, appoint each
                offender a governor's position in
                a southern prison. Just do it,
                we'll be in contact soon.

                Oh, and John, make sure we give
                them all a suit!

Ryan

Suicidal Youth

There is a pandemic upon us.
One that has covered the planet
and ravaged many lives.
Though don't be eluded
for I am not talking of the one
currently dancing on humanity's lips,
painted on every front-page headline.

The subject on my mind is nowhere near visible.
But unseen doesn't mean unreal
for the most fatal predators are the silent ones.
And nescient is the person who overlooks this.
The pandemic I speak of is a stygian one.
Such a taboo
that most sufferers sew their own lips together
with threads of okays
in fear of discovery.

That pain is often preferrable to the truth being unearthed.
They keep up this facade until one day these lies form a
noose
that they don't even notice until it's around their neck.
But it's too late then because it was society that left them
for dead.

Phoenix

Just Beyond the Wire

I hadn't meant to have
a conversation with the flower.
It just happened.

A small, rather ragged, foxglove
stunted, struggling next to the fence.
I felt sorry for it.

After all, Jonah was redeemed
in the eyes of God when he felt
sorry for a withering plant

Talking to plants is a way
to see ahead. You have to
really listen to their replies –

Whispers on the vagaries of wind, and
a flowing murmur of juices pumping up
from their roots.

And their reactions
to the probing of insects.
Listen and you will find answers.

Anonymous

The Man with the Flute

A Man sat in his Cell one day
and wrote this poem, what can I say
So where did he find his inspiration from
Covid 19 and self-isolation.

One day he was bored, so he gave a frown,
thought won't let this beat me, or get me down
Now Stuck on my own, my voice was on mute
I think I will buy, and leam to play a flute

Now some months on, and I'm getting there
Sweet melodic tunes now fill the air
Edelweiss and Annie's Song,
some played right, some played wrong.

Like a penny whistle, bagpipe playing wailer,
Sometimes I have to use my inhaler.
In time I hope, sometimes I pray
I'll sound just like that James Galway

So you can see that man I'd like to be
is the man with the flute, and that Man is me!

N

Steeldoor Studio

Anonymous

James

OUT OF A PRISON OF BODY
INTO A PRISON OF MIND
OUT FROM A PLACE MORE CERTAIN
INTO A PLACE LESS KIND

Marylin

Going through things
you never thought
you'd go through

Will take you places
you never thought
you'd get to.

Malcolm

Home

This house was never a home: The day we moved in someone had written "RUN WHILE YOU CAN", in green chalk on the wall.

This house was never safe: Neighbours came, disguised as friends. With fake kindness and generosity. They bought 'gifts' in the form of flea infested carpets, and broken furniture. With blatant cruelty and intimidation, they terrorised my kids.

This house did not hold peace: It bought years of constant striving to escape my past. I tried to prove myself, improve myself, and show the doubters they were wrong. It bought heartbreak, as everyone I loved either died, or walked away.

Now I sit within these walls. This empty shell, undecorated, ugly and neglected, I feel like the walls have become a part of me, a reflection of my failures, and broken dreams.

Old habits beckon like a familiar friend. With a wave and a cheeky grin, mocking me with promises of comfort, friendship and escape. I know they can't keep the promises, but they are comfortable and tempting all the same.

I sometimes long to jump into the familiar embrace of oblivion.

Global uncertainty enlightens minds. Suddenly population control is plausible, and conspiracies believable.

It frightens me, because what am I? Collateral damage? Disposable?

I'm someone who lived when I should have died. Let's face it, I'm a shadow in other people's lives. Who phones me first? Who checks on me for my sake?

I'm an afterthought at best and at worst an obligation. I contribute nothing to the world so who would really miss me?

It's a question that will always go unanswered, because when voiced, it's dismissed before it's begun. Its validity is diminished by harsh words, a roll of the eyes, and a flap of the hand.

But despite all my sadness, and the dark thoughts in my mind, I do have hope and gratitude for new beginnings.

This temporary silence, this pause in our universal existence will end one day. Life is changing, new heroes are emerging, and the earth is healing. Could it be that a new world is waiting with open arms, to welcome us home?

Debbie

Desesperación

What is lived will always, eventually, become history, poetry, legend or myth. But putting those moments into words is not easy, especially when you realise that you are stuck in an abyss, a nightmare, and you might not get out. You try to stand and face your own destiny, but it is hard not to bend to your own fears, to your monsters and phantoms.

Homeless, without identity, a stranger in a foreign land, you walk like a pariah and you feel reduced. Your people, your family and friends, feel so far away from you. The communities where you belonged are not for you anymore. You feel like everything was a lie, a fraud, that you are alone against this world. You knock on doors, but they close in your face. You get sad and do not care about anything. Fatigue invades you, making you forget even your hunger. You think about suicide, about the earth swallowing you. You walk without strength, starving, dirty and breathless, under shadows, awaiting the worst.

You share affection with some of the dogs you meet in the street. They understand your pain. Lay by your side. And you wonder: 'what did I do to deserve this?' You torture yourself asking when it is going to stop? You cry out: 'my God, my God, why have you forsaken me? Help me. Forgive me. I cannot continue like this.'

It is in this lowest moment, when you have surrendered absolutely, that someone you do not know touches your shoulder and speaks to you: 'my friend, do not cry. I have been through this too, you are not alone. I will help you.' You want to protect yourself, get angry or ignore that person. But instead you listen and he gives you the address of a place where they will treat you worthily and give you basic services like a shower, food, and laundry.

He shakes your hand and says: 'cheer up and go.' In that moment of farewell, you look up at the sky, and make up your mind.

Luis
Translated from Spanish by Felipe

In this Together

We are all
In this together,
The unconnected,
The uncultured,

There are free lessons for the uneducated.
You can't clean hospital toilets from home.
You can't keep two meters apart on packed public transport.

We are all
In this together,
We are separate but not separated,
We are in isolation but not alone.

The poor people working back-to-back shifts
Looking after those that have become surplus
to requirement
For you we will clap
And now that most the shops are closed
Your minimum wage should last longer
See there's good news.

The government's turned the closed down hotels
into prisons for the homeless
And set up a task force
To look into the reason that people in ethnic communities
Are dying in much higher numbers than the rest of us.

The big cover up
The use of facemasks could be made compulsory
You can now hide your big Cheshire grin

As you push your overloaded trolley
Past your elderly neighbours
As they walk bent double
In overcoat and gardening gloves
Searching for their milk and porridge.

We are all
in this together
We have started to say hello to one another
But more in a way of warning than a friend
Keep two chevrons apart

Things may be getting back to normal
They say
We are getting on top of this
But we need to be careful
And try to avoid the
Second spike.

Gary

Mushy Pea Friday

Day One of Fear

Being held in isolation against my will. Basically like every other day.

Panic set in after 3 hours. No food, no drink. Then I remembered I had a tap and a flapjack. Whew!

But as I was eating it: emergency! A crumb slid down into dressing gown. I was naked underneath to preserve precious clothes supply and it settled somewhere only lovers should see. Don't judge me but I still ate it. In times of trouble, are we not all capable of savage acts of barbarism?

I imagine support marches across the UK have started. They do worry about us.

Just been told enforced exercise is at 2.15: this punishment just gets worse.

Day Four – No end in sight

The mind games have started. The enforced exercise was an hour earlier today! They don't realise that I know. That I can measure time. I place one kidney bean (didn't work with baked beans) on top of another until they reach the ceiling and that is one hour.

They have painted lines on the ground outside, clearly measuring our walking speed and to listen in to our plans. I've heard rumours the vegetables are clumps of sand painted bright colours.

I was granted a brief audience with head honcho peeker today. He tried to recruit me to write propaganda for his peekers. Said he would love to read it and sign it. Always one step ahead – they just want to know my thoughts.

Day Thirty – Wednesday I Believe

I am writing this on Thursday, but as it is entitled Wednesday that means I can be prophetic and positive and announce that tomorrow does indeed exist! Hurrah! I seem to be writing in the style of a poor lowly jester of the 18th century. Have I lost my mind? Whispered conversations heard outside my steel barricade. Fortunately my unicorn Melons helps me remain grounded and calm.

Day Forty-Two – Monday Mayhem

This is madness. I don't know how they do it but the peekers have managed to remove the May Day bank holiday from the calendar. This must be a sign of their ever increasing power. Melons is sulking. Enforced exercise was early today. I rode around on Melons for half an hour. No one noticed. She still wants a humbug.

Day Forty Seven – Time Has Ceased

I am starting to talk to penguins. I don't know how they cope with the heat. Melons tells me I am imagining them, but what does she know? She might be gorgeous, but she is not the brightest. A rumour is going around that a peeker is missing. Will investigate.

Day Sixty – No Way Day Sixty – Aargg!

I made it. Battled away to 60. Not my age – I might not make that – but the amount of days various peekers have used ingenious ways to destroy me. Each sweep of my comb reminds me of passing time as each silvery thread flutters and falls to the floor like an anorexic snowflake. They went to far today. Mushy pea Friday was stolen from us. They replaced our mushy peas with something so evil I can hardly bear to bring myself to write it. They replaced my beloved mushy peas with – sobs – peas! Can you believe it? The fiendish foes.'

Steve

Weather the Storm

Were you alone?
Did you miss me?
Are you stranded now upon a shore built from a fresh
fear
As we re-emerge?

Still the anxious fluttering within your heart and listen to
the echoes of the storm,
The aftermath of it is fading in the song of the moments
it created.
Moments now that tell of a new hope, a new touch,
A new us.

In the weathering we have forged a chain of creativity
that has hugged the world and
broken down barriers, walls of despair.
Don't let its chains break now.

In the weathering we have shared, opening both hearts
and ears
To electronic channels and new communications,
Found new ways to find our peace, and in the search,
new connections.

As the storm's roar fades, we need not be in contact
every day, every week, every month;
Let's not pressure ourselves as we did before to be 'on'

and 'doing' every second.

But at the breath of every moment let's remember this
new-found touch of humanity,
This glimmer of light in the darkest of days.

Let's not forget how that feels,
And in our emergence from these constraints
Remember we were distant but physically, not socially.

This is our time to show that Humanity, and its sibling
Empathy, can endure.
Let's not waste this precious gift of time and reflection.
Make the change and speak your peace for all to hear.

Leena

New Normal

Years we've been steering clear of the block
But now it feels like we're back in that compound
My headspace awash with negativity
In particular it's the fears I can't block out.

I was due to finish therapy in a couple of months
My inner-voice weeping to me – 'maybe not now'
Don't count your chickens before they've hatched
I hear the sound of my dreams being shot down.

Meanwhile I'm in a prison system
on furlough
I've lost all structure with the late nights
By three in the afternoon I'm ready to conk out.

I now binge on junk food
living real feral like I'm in a dog pound
festering in the fragrance of flatulence
But never put off at the sight of food

To arrest the slide I know I need exercise
But I know I don't wanna squat now or either weigh train
I'm past the point where I have a choice
This idle behaviour has led to serious weight gain

Telling my daughter I love her
and to stay safe.

Emotionally unloading to my keyworker
Though not too deeply – this isn't a 'safe space'.

The content of the convo entails me taking responsibility
Because no longer do I point fingers or place blame
I strive to figure out how to father successfully
My child's closer to getting indicted than an A grade.

If I'd have been free I'd have been marching in the streets
for a movement that's accelerating faster than race pace
I take a knee with the protesters, activists, and dreamers
for the discriminated, segregated, lynched, and enslaved

Shaun

Virtually There

In a cast-off remark, the lad from Gogglebox states the Coronavirus 'lockdown' makes him feel like a prisoner, because he only gets exercise for forty minutes and a shower a day. Well, apart from the fact that he got it wrong with his assumption that we've retained the right to exercise and shower daily, he underestimates how an inmate may be feeling whilst confined in a cell for over twenty-three hours a day. At the moment it is not so much that prisoners are shut up, but that they are shut out.

Residents are feeling alienated from the 'all in it together' community spirit that seems to be binding their communities, and increasingly severed from the family unit. It's a potent reminder of your sins, as part of societies supposed criminal underclass, when you're not able to be integral to collective effort. Prisoners are feeling like a burden as keyworkers risk their health to look after us.

Thoughts like this can have a profound effect on a man's desire to rehabilitate. Absence makes the heart grow fonder, but isolation makes the mind go weaker. It is proven that a major factor in encouraging an ex-offender to desist from crime is his continuing ability to interact with his family. The Farmer Report called for family members to be treated as 'valued allies in the rehabilitation cause', and recognised that pro-social interactions with significant others are fundamental if people are to change. So it follows that a sensible compromise is to deny an offender his liberty, but to facilitate visits to maintain his family ties.

Inmates have recognised the protective measures are for their own protection. And so it would be a valuable reciprocation of our cooperation if the justice system could keep families in touch. There's no doubt the world has changed irrevocably during lockdown. Ordinary citizens have their freedom restricted and are exposed to levels of isolation comparable to prisoners. But while technology allows free-folk to adapt their everyday interactions, that hasn't happened in prisons. The question begs: if video technology can enable the process of incarceration by facilitating remote court hearings, then why can it not safeguard these indispensable family ties?

Of the men I speak to, the overwhelming fear is that their children may feel 'out of sight, out of mind' or abandoned. Others simply shared feelings of insecurity.

Some common sense has prevailed. Phone credit in lieu of lost visits was a sensible adjustment, especially as telephone charges have finally been reduced to enable less frantic, time-pressured calls. The consensus is that prisons have done a good job in mirroring the precautions taken in society and responding well to the Covid-19 threat. However, elsewhere the world has been kept sane by interacting via Portal and staying connected through Zoom. Countries such as Italy and Finland utilise Skype, and Catalonian prisons have adapted WhatsApp. Northern Ireland introduced video calls within the first month of lockdown. Some would protest that we are guilty of procrastination at a time when the rest of the world is embracing change. Even in a Covid-free world the benefits would be too numerous to ignore. Not only would foreign nationals be able to communicate with family, but so would others that struggle to stay in touch due to distance, old-age, or infirmity.

Prisons must now accept that the wellbeing of its residents is imperative. We must embrace the latest technology to keep in touch.

Jonathan

The Unknown

It was hard watching a different reality on TV. People visiting seaside and parks whilst we only had 10 minutes out.

But do you know what the hardest thing was? Living in the unknown. What will happen? Why? How?

I wish somebody had made an attempt to explain, just to talk to us.

Feeling powerless was killing.

Harrison

A Mother's Pain

My son is currently serving a nine-year sentence.

As Covid-19 spreads across the country and the world at a devastating rate, you can imagine my anguish and heartache, nobody seems to care about.

My last contact with my son was on Mother's Day, 22 March 2020. The memory of when we were able to celebrate it together in freedom, keeps me going through the pain and anxiety of not being able to see him since then.

It has been very hard to connect to our loved ones inside to fully understand how this experience is impacting them. Our conversations are guarded and filled with only small talks of weather, children, gym, food... Neither of us wants to share a real pain of the damage that Covid -19 is causing to us. We are trying to protect each other from more harm by not speaking about it at all.

Those of us outside can take for granted that we can pick up the phone or jump on a zoom call and talk to our loved ones. But with prisoners it's not so easy.

My son is in a Cat D estate. He has worked very hard to reach this stage into his long sentence and he truly earned those small benefits that come with it: home leave, day release opportunity to work outside and hope to begin the journey of reintegration. All of his dreams have been frozen in space and time. And mine too.

He reads and watches the news how Covid-19 affects BAME communities, then feels more anxious as little is being done to discuss or reassure BAME prisoners. This lack of communication, internally and externally, reaffirms our feeling that for the service and the society, we mean nothing.

My son is lucky to be in a Cat D prison during the pandemic. He has earned his own cell and

The prison provides outside gym activity, albeit very limited, which amounts a lot during these difficult times. He is thankful we are able to provide funds, so he can purchase extra cleaning equipment instead of food to protect himself from the virus. Vast majority of prisons do not have same benefits and my heart goes out to those who cannot read or write to maintain contact or have funds to ring and talk.

All we can do is to be there for continuous support, unconditional love and become their counsellors when it gets beyond the pain. We can provide hope for future, not only for our loved ones in prisons but also their children, their partners and other members of our families.

But who is there for us, mums? Who cares for me?

Sharon

Locked In

I spent most of my youth and a part of my adult life, locked down.

After two or three times, it's like riding a bike. Once I got my head around it, it's a piece of cake – this lockup experience. You don't have to deal with no one, worry about bills, or anything other than trying to get a joint or a line of smack.

I thought I could ride lockdown in HMP stylee.

6.30am Gail stirs for work. I'm awake. "Morning love," I say.

I go and relieve myself, get back under the quilt, my phone vibrates.

How many brain numbing conversations on the phone am I expected to have? I pick it up and check the book face, "Friends" doing perfect stuff. Oh look, there's some home schooling going on with that most dysfunctional family.

I can see my daughter's called last night.

"Gary, coffee's ready if you want it," Gail shouts.

I'm genuinely happy for a hot moment.

"Thank you darling," I say. But I wonder, is that going to be my moment? Out of the 1440 minutes of the next 24 hours. Is that the single moment of happiness?

I watch BBC 24 on a loop for two hours. "We're fucked," I mumble and then admonish myself for watching the news. Then I admonish myself for admonishing myself.

There's the phone again. The pre-selected ringtone tells me it's my daughter, Danielle. I love Danielle.

I can't bring myself to answer. What would I ask? "Hi babe, you ok? Kids ok?" I tell myself of course they're ok, they're always ok every time I ask. I could have chatted to my grandkids on facetime. I love my grandkids.

But the phone stops ringing with an accusing silence. And the day stretches out before me. Nothing to do. And nowhere I can go.

You get the picture.

I know what lockdown I prefer.

Gary

Hello

Do you know who I am?
I've been struggling for a while
I see you from the window
And I always raise a smile

There you go again
Rushing in every way
I'd come out to my door
But what would I say?

Hello, I'm your neighbour
Lived here twenty years
Could I trouble you for help
Until I get over my fears?

I had a fall not so long ago
And I'm scared to leave my home
I don't have any support around
And I live here on my own

But why would I trouble you
You don't even know my name
Not enough time in your day
Your routine always the same

I'll continue to smile from my window
Reminded of how my life used to be
And maybe you'll stop for a moment
You might just see me

Kirsty

23-11

Can you begin to see,
what life must be like for me?
As Lockdown restrictions ease, you become more free
But will you spare a thought for me?
11 weeks on and I'm still barged-up for 23 hours a day
So will you listen to what I we got to say?

I'm used to being locked in my 'home' – this is
my normal
The pandemic just made things more formal
At one time there wasn't much between us, you know
Please think differently now, looking through my cell
window.

Anonymous

Consequences

Before the lockdown
I would be there with her.
Happy as can be.
Spend the weekend together,
She'd say 'please stay with me.'

During the lockdown
She would cut her arms.
She would feel alone.
She would be depressed.
No-one would have known.

Before the lockdown
we'd go Saturday shopping.
And we'd go for a walk
maybe out for a drive
She'd call me a 'silly dork.'

During the lockdown
She would cut her arms.
She would feel alone.
She would be depressed.
No-one would have known.

Before the lockdown
I'd buy her Sunday lunch,
or she'd cook me pasta.

When I'd go to work
She'd wish the week would go faster.

During the lockdown
She would cut her arms.
She would feel alone.
She would be depressed.

No-one would have known.
Before the lockdown
the weekend would come.
We'd have such a laugh
taking lots of selfies,
and going to the café.

During the lockdown
She'd grab the pills.
Just like so.
On route to hospital.
Now we all know.

During this lockdown
you can still be near
And we will get through this
Despite the fear

So when it's time to talk
step up to the plate.
Because you will regret it
when it becomes too late.

Check on those you love.
Email and telephone.
Plan for life after lockdown.
No more time alone.

Jack

Oxygen

It surrounds you and I, like fog, A thick, engulfing, swallowing fog

The funny thing about fog, though, is that it fades away Breaks apart like curtains at the start of a performance Even then, the show must end.

The curtains close. The fog swallows us again like a nefarious beast

Your candle blown out.

But candles can be relit.

James

Afterword

In 2005 I was asked to run some creative writing classes for a charity working with people in recovery in Boscombe. I was supposed to do 10 weeks and ended up staying for 10 years because I couldn't leave: I loved the voices so much, and found the writers as talented and smart as any I had worked with in any university or organisation. Week after week I found myself taken aback by the freshness of the writing, and the openness and generosity of the writers in our workshop.

16 years later I am still working with unheard voices. It's vital that all voices are heard, and that we have a record of how the pandemic has affected all of society. That's why Paperchains is so important.

Talent is everywhere: I have stumbled across it in all corners of the world. I am haunted by a young Inuit woman in Labrador, whose writing was clear and beautiful, and by a young Roma girl who wrote a story of her family's relationship with their performing bear. I can't help all of those people tell their stories, but we organisations can do something.

We need to make sure that opportunity is not a privilege, that we work in communities to identify and support talented people, including people who don't even know that they have talent. We need to make work of the highest quality and never patronise.

People need to see themselves represented, to realise doors are open for them. We need to redistribute power, so more people have access to make and watch work. We need to learn how to support outsider voices so that they don't fall at hurdles, because that will allow those with connections and privileged backgrounds to dominate the arts.

But most of all, we need these voices out in the world because they are brilliant and refreshing and tell us new stories and teach us new ways of seeing the world. They bridge gaps between us and make us all more human.

Nell

Acknowledgements

Paperchains is the work of many people, not just those whose work is included in this anthology. We would like to thank everyone who submitted work, and to all the people who read and responded so generously to the entries.

Thank you to Arts Council, England for supporting this anthology and the show that brings it to life. We couldn't do what we do without the work Arts Council, England does to facilitate and fund creativity for all.

Finally, for lending all these writers your ears, eyes, and attention, thank you dear readers.

Paperchains was honoured to have the support of the following people and organisations

Authors: Lucy Brett, Melvin Burgess, Martina Cole, Cressida Cowell, Miranda Dickinson, Anthony Horowitz,

Christopher Impey, Stephen Kelman, Russ Litten, Clare Mackintosh, Tom Palmer, Ian Thornton.

Organisations & Publications: Army & You Magazine, BBC Radio, BBFC, BFBS Radio, The Big Issue, The Bookseller, Cambridge University Press, Hay Festival, Help for Heroes, Inside Time, Loud & Clear, National Prison Radio, RAF Families Federation, SSAFA, Scragends Literary Agency, Soldier Magazine, Transforming Communities Together, Wild Pressed Books, YMCA Open Door.

Individuals: HRH The Duchess of Cornwall, David Austin, Alan Birch, Christopher Bone, Justyn Caie, Gina Carter, Laura Cartledge, Clifford Caswell, Mark Chandler, Suzanne Chislett, Jo Crocker, Michael Curran, Degard, Sarah Dove, Charlotte Eadie, Alice Farrow, Stephen Fry, Emma Goswell, Verity Geere, Victoria Gray, Faye Harcourt, James Henderson, John Henderson, Erwin James, Philip Jones, Piers Linney, Lachlan Macara, Felipe Durán Martínez. Paul McNamee, Heidi Mulvey, Rebecca Perry, Robert Plant, Susanne Rose, Lisa Shattock, Julia Silk, Martin Spain, Chris Vallance, John Vincent, Deborah Walton, Robert Whitehouse, Scott Whitehouse, Andrew Wilkie, Terry Williamson, Caroline Woodward, and Lucy Wray.

Thank you for supporting planet-friendly publishing

Story Machine seeks to have a net positive social and environmental impact. That means the environment and people's lives are actually better off for every book we print. Story Machine offsets our entire carbon footprint plus 10% through a www.ClimateCare.org programme. We are now investing in converting to use only 100% renewable energies and seeking out the most planet-positive means of shipping books to our readers.

The printing insustry is a huge polluter, requiring the use of huge amounts of water, toxic chemicals, and energy. Even FSC certified mix paper sources drive deforestation. That's why we are proud to be working with www.Seacort.net, a global leader in planet positive printing. Not only have they developed a waterless and chemical-free process, they use only 100% renewable energies, FSC certified recycled paper, and direct absolutely no waste to landfill. That's why they were crowned Europe's most sustainable SME in 2017, and have been recognised as one of the top three environmental printers in the world.

Planet-positive printing costs us a little more. But we think this is a small price to pay for a better world, today and in the future. If you agree, please share our message, and encourage other publishers and authors to commit to planet-positive printing. Stories can change the world. They deserve publishers that want to make sure they do. Together, we can make publishing more sustainable.